LACE
THROWN OVER
UNVARNISHED
DEATH
(POEMS)

Krys Call

This book is meant to serve as a companion to those humans who are grieving for another human. It is dedicated to every human who grieves for another human and to those for whom they grieve. A previous book of poems, *Seedpod and Other Poems for Meditation* includes poems about the difficult process of grieving for nonhuman animals.

Acknowledgements
Thanks to Bernice Graham and to Dr. Sherdeen Graham for their friendship, generosity and kindness. Thanks to Paula Till for her own generosity in doing careful reading and giving useful literary advice to me for decades.

TABLE OF CONTENTS

A Note to the Departed

It's unclear down here
how to correctly
and effectively grieve.
Words don't seem to work.
Terms can no more
meld love, regret, hope, and loss
into a consummately final phrase
than could a gap-toothed collection
of worn wooden alphabet blocks.

Grief seems to be
a *concerto grosso*
in three parts
baroquely based
upon the assumption
that the contention
between memory
and the emptied now
will become an accord
by the time the opening themes
return in the *rondeau,*
a final agreement
between the mind's
notions of past and present
being hinted at along the way
by accidentals
which, bit by little bit,
resolve minutely
into the tonic.

But during the slow second movement
of grief's *concerto da chiesa,*
when time elongates at the event horizon
in the starlit foyer
of the concert hall
where sounds
the finale,
we, the grieving,
may come apart,
falling away faster
than the movement can end.
Some of our thoughts disperse,
atomizing into meaningless distractions
of grace notes,
other notions temporarily hanging together
as well-worn sixteenth note runs
singing kitsch imaginings of a quaint hereafter.
Memories are wrenched
and extracted in pieces,
those still-warm fragments cast
into the searing cold
of a dramatically sudden
orchestral silence.

It could be that grief is a piece
which, for some of us,
is too hard to play.
Perhaps it is a composition
that can't be executed
using only willingness,
a self-tuned instrument,
and technically correct hand positions.

Our neural networks
may possess an incapacity.
Perhaps an electrical hairnet
woven of tiny bursts
of red and blue light
cannot accurately map
the narrow shelf left at the edge
of the recently crumbled cliff
where you dropped off
into infinity.
In the end,
it appears that grieving
is not something that we do,
but something that does us.

Yet even if I could,
I would not call you back
from your nested warmth
in a shadowed indigo fold
of the Mother's starry cloak.
Nor would I interrupt
the banquet where you elegantly dine
on the green sprigs of graces
that you journeyed
far across our world to find.

But I will tell you
that our world's
tiniest ungulate,
the mouse deer
(weighing fewer
than ten pounds),

was recently discovered alive
and is being protected
in faraway China.

I will not ask you to wait for me,
to stay where you rest above
the lavishly vast aqua of crystal seas
over whose unrumpling contours
of epipelagic waves
the rising sun is cooing
a single peach-hued
whole note.
I will not beseech you
to avoid reincarnation
until I can see you again
as I asked that favor
for his own safety
of my luckless yellow cat.
Meanwhile, it is clear even here
that your ever-rising eyebeams
are raising the rafters of heaven
and that your glowing joy
is increasing the womblike wideness
of its lavender vault.

I want to thank you
for the hydrothermic vent field
that arose
from a crinkling crevasse
which cracked open
between
two slowly retreating

tectonic plates of time
and released generative heat burbling
in low, slow arpeggios,
intoning magma's
creation song.
The steam of it
began to wisp
in the moment
when you stepped
down
carefully
into the most
dangerous corner
of our neighborhood
much as the mouse deer
places tentative hooves
between slim shadows,
stepping inside
stretched diamond outlines
laid across curled umber leaves
lying at the base of the cold
steel chain-linked fence of extinction.

You already know everything I want to say,
but clock time is the place where
we, the dying,
are allowed and obliged
to read aloud from our *exercices orales.*
Therefore, it is now
the hour to thank you
for what you have shown us
of life in the land of the fully alive.

It is the time as well
to thank our friend
whose indelible mark
on the obverse
dignifies the thumb-worn
coin of my soul,
and who also made
soft, leaf-caressed
sunlight to glow
against the hidden side,
showing the reverse surface
to be stamped as well.

When you stepped down
from the curb
of a perilous intersection
in this place loud
with Hallowe'en-hued muscle cars,
with carnivorously growling trucks,
and ascream with spates of speed
briefly semicoloned
in breakneck wheelies
recklessly risked
by sharp-nosed
mosquito motorbikes,
and you offered a polite "Hello,"
the ghostly coin which had been
dithering as loose change
in some numinous Area 51
under my sternum
turned around,
the wafer and wight

of that patina'd quiddity
revealing its reverse.

About a year later,
when you spoke more,
that same century coin,
borrowing illumination
from the radiantly gilded green light
of our friend's fern-laced spring,
proved to have been hand struck
on the reverse with an image
of soft-lobed hearts laced together
as would choral voices twine *ad libitum,*
the clear and obscure,
the winging and deep, turning,
melting into each other
in a *bhakti kirtan*
interweaving devotion with creation
to lyrically compose your face.

Death

Death is a line
drawn in the mind
between a remembered moment
when slender, eyebrow-shaped leaves
made shell sounds
as they moved sideways against each other
as wind shimmied through
branches
adangle
over
gravity of Earth,
breezes swathing the air with scents
of eucalyptus and mulching apple leaves,
and this one:
it is an undotted line drawn
between certain previous moments
and now.

Chinese elm
and blue gum trees knew your step,
gently insistent, as if following a light.
I could almost see it
several squares of sidewalk ahead of us,
a lucent orb levitating at a level
with your furrowed brow.
But the nimbus of it was dimmed
by the ruckus of the street,
by the call to chaos
of diesel pipes chortling,
that sound ripping

the cardboard day
which was formed of small,
uniform corrugations,
each regular loop
of thick, brown paper
another minute elapsed
as we walked uphill
to achieve the sloping strip mall
that begins with a pub
on the corner,
then a pet food store,
then a dead chicken parts store,
and after that,
your destination, the United Parcel Service
just this side of the hardware store
where the workers wear loose, red drover's vests.

As you leaned into your near future at the UPS,
the wind found the wide brim
of your cream cotton *chapeau.*
Flung and fallen flat onto the sidewalk,
it was a hat deflated by the loss of its head.
Bending and swooping down
with one swinging arm to pick it up,
I recalled having done so
more than a century ago.

You are gone
and out of sight now,
and in the humidor aromatic of cedar
wherein months of the year
are arranged in rows of twelve

like fine cigars
and the air of the self is kept sequestered
from that of the world,
this is what there is:
a few of these moments of hat and sidewalk,
of you laughing
on a dun-hued bench
made of recycled plastic bottles
in front of the fluted pillars
of the Carnegie library,
of you stepping off the corner
in the long red dress
with the white lace down the front,
and of you on that same corner,
clothed in pink layers
and matching winter gloves,
standing still
all by yourself
just looking at my house.
By the time I got outside,
you were already gone.

In the cedar-lined
Bird's Eye Maple humidor,
these flat photos of the mind
are stacked on
the top row of months
which were your last,
the faded pictures arranged
in order of time.
Under the dry images,
lying on its back,

is a round, clear glass container
containing the distillation
of an auditory mirror occurrence.
The liquid within is the current
which irrigated
the chakra under my ribs
whenever you were on the phone.
Then I could hear
luminescent juice runneling
in the chlorophyllous
longitudinal grooves of your voice,
a rustic-edged, soft sound,
as if it were an early morn in creation,
and mushroom-tongued salamanders
were raising flat, inquisitive heads
from slanting-down hills
of broad, elliptical allspice leaves
shading amphoraelike
their sweetshrub fruits
while skinks stretched their
curled cobalt tongues
toward a vaporous veil
behind which branches and wind
were beginning to talk,
the moist-skinned lizards
tasting tiny droplets
in the lifting mist,
sensing the enlivening scent
of something hidden
and asurge,
something
moving upward

through xylems,
the unnamed
liquor of life
rising
through
chartreuse
sapwood.
And then all around and above,
there was an exuberant soft-feathered rustling
as pliant-branched Dawn Redwoods unruffled
the umbrellas of their first, sky-splashing crowns.

On the Phone

From thousands of miles away,
your mother calls
to ask how I am
and to tell me about you
as you once were.
It is as if together
under a darkening dome of indigo
from which light is fast recessing,
in the infinite blue of our evening of grieving,
we're asquat on the ground,
warming ourselves
at the fire of your life.
She throws in kindling sticks-
the names of the countries you visited,
the states where you went to school,
what you would and wouldn't eat.
As we hunker down
in the cold of our advancing night,
she points out
the larger branches in the blaze-
your work as a doctor,
your academic degrees,
and the two men you nearly married.
She leaves an envelope
in my mailbox
with her address written
on it in blue ballpoint pen.
It contains one photograph
and quiet air.
In the picture,

you are young and healthy
and standing at ease.
Behind you is a cumulus effusion of green,
a small tree flowering
with lemon-yellow trumpet blooms.
Some palm branches to your left reach
companionably toward it.
When I ask,
she explains about the dress
whose lacy thinness
rests peacefully
on the spareness of your frame.
She says that because of the climate in Grenada,
those who can afford it wear white.
All that she says is new.
You were not one
to talk about yourself
and especially not of your accomplishments.
Instead, you spoke worriedly
of the voluntary enslavement
of humans to technology.
We also discussed colors:
you loved soft shades and
and layers of translucencies,
aqua seas and evening skies of turquoise,
sunrises of rose and peach.
You talked to me about words.
Once you pointed to a printed page,
the pad of your finger touching
the dark raised ink of the word "elegiac."
Now, here, everything is elegy.
Your white dress,

and the scarlet one
with the white lace trim,
the innumerable layers
of cotton and wool that you wore in winter,
the citric scent of lemon oil
always encircling you,
your calm, considering glance,
your soft downward sigh,
your warm, surprised laugh
casting a fan of golden green
droplets of nectar
into the sonic void,
your solar flares of thought,
all have now been archived
between algebraic parentheses
as a closed set of iconographic attributes
taken from you by us
because we need them more.
They now have been solidified,
flattened, leafed in gold, and carefully captioned
with seriffed calligraphy by hyperbolizing love,
the anecdotal having been turned symbolic.
As you turn your stride away from us,
messengers
clothed as Monarch butterflies
are seen afloat
in your back draft,
angling their wings
as they approach us,
flying strangely low.
Did you also send the dream
wherein you told me

that you had given birth,
and that the child had died?
Your mother says that it isn't so.
I awake to find something
slumped on the floor by my bed.
It is a metaphoric canvas knapsack
torn by time, worn a little by regret,
and almost empty.
It carries two photographs
and some sounds,
the Great Mother sung
in *bhajans* composed
of tropical hues of light
and the speaking silence
of words you texted to me
which are still on my phone.
The pack settles itself easily on my back.
The straps pulling back on my shoulders
tell me that the past tense and I
now belong to one another.
On the trail, I look down
at the rubbled sturdiness
of a tilted stratum of pale marble
crossing under the footpath's rusty clay,
at the slick vein of metamorphic stone
that has been exposed by
a cold, slanting rain.
As I feel the small explosions
of dried chunks of red earth
powdering to dust under my boots,
you walk on in another,
unencumbered now.

Spring

In February, Spring is already afoot.
Trees and bushes,
having realized that
another California drought is coming,
send the water
cisterned by their xylem
into new, green shoots.
Out in the side yard,
daffodil trumpets converse daily
with ripe, planet-shaped lemons.
And the faces
of sunny yellow *oxalis luteola,*
newly unfolded,
stretch on thin stems
from their clover bed
to chime in.
It seems that green things are too busy to talk,
but that yellow flowers and fruit,
already having attained their apotheoses,
cannot repress their good spirits and gregariousness.
This is the spring when you were to be well:
it is easy to imagine you walking in the sun.
But without you, the year,
humming to itself
in a machinelike way,
proprietarily rolls out its days,
each of which
makes the most of itself;
under burgeoning illumination,
each noon's transparent lens of sky

refracts and magnifies time.

And the sun,
stroking them like fur,
makes much
of the proliferation
of little green grasses.
There is a sussurant rushing
of soughing breezes
who never stop speaking
in the vibrating harp strings
of draping eucalypti
or calling gutterally
through tilting
towers of tall
and naked poplars
who are awkwardly
but patiently awaiting
their own verdant vesture.
The rushing sound
increases to a roar
as those breezes
speak more hurriedly
of fruition to come.
Coastal fog,
preferring muted mornings
when the single coo of a dove
appears notated upon heavy mist
as in plainchant,
as an oblong black dot,
finding itself faced
with talkative noons

full of bustle and rustling of the wind,
and the pouncing upon ends of leafy branches
by vocally embattled birds,
becomes discouraged.
The fog recedes,
seeking its own solitude
under the horizon.

Segments of sidewalk
whose strenuous efforts
can never bring them
any farther than just
around the block
gradually
look larger
and more whitish
as weekdays of winter daylight
lengthen into rectangles,
becoming blank parcels
of time on the calendar.
But in the butter-churning
auric blossoming of spring,
and in the puddling out
into shimmering mirage
of summer's solar light,
you are still here.

In the blast of noon,
you're present
as a contemplative listening,
a folding in the middle distance,
the sky seemingly

having taken a tuck in itself.
You are not so much a shadow
as a more gathered light
It is the pale, vibrant blue
of the twilight scent
of night-blooming jasmine,
a fluent liquid hue
quietly coursing
under a darker shade
of indigo silence
that is slowly
falling to earth
as it does
at the coming
of each new night,
when in the age-old
processional,
detachedly
from a distance,
the heliosphere
formally loves
glossy lemon leaves
with massless silk
of moonlight.

The Year

Dressed in black skinny jeans
and a matching turtleneck,
gripping in his right hand
a takeout cappuccino
in a white cardboard cup,
the modern Julian year
paces ahead
on ruled spaces
of sidewalk.

Turning left at the
corner of Christmas,
taking a short leg
along the railroad tracks,
he invigorates himself
by quaffing his coffee
on New Year's Day.
Coming to where
the tracks meet the street,
on Valentine's Day
he crinkles his scruff
with a crooked,
come-hither smile
at Primavera's
nubile form.
Then he turns left
again
and steps
onto a smooth
segment of cement,

passing without caring
about the loss of it
the place that was once
a garter snake habitat
composed of long, green, wild grasses.
It is now a cement-aproned
row of shoebox houses
hunched cheek by jowl,
slowly chewing
on their first mortgages.
Without stopping,
he leans into
springtime's
downhill stretch
toward summer,
shaking his Roman curls
in a March rain so light
that it is almost dew.
Stride by stride
he comes down
the sidewalk
toward our house,
but without you.

When we turn away
from his caffeinated chatter
and from the visual shout
of his jazzy, uncombed hair, backlit as it is
by a glorious noonday sun,
we find that you are still here,
your spare form
appearing above us

in lavender silhouette.
Gazing downward
and off to the side
consideringly,
silently attentive,
here you are,
freestanding in midair.

Understood

If you have things to do,
and you need to move on
and away from us,
I am guessing
that we all understand.
You once texted me
that prayer is
the most important thing.
We hear that prayer is popular
among those who now,
in traditional metaphoric terms,
glide on gilded wings
a hands-breadth over
roseate drifts of surfeit joy,
or on foot, who wander rain-washed
grassy landscapes pastoral
or stroll the sun-warmed stones
of glowing citadels
of the storied hereafter,
or who quietly abide
in the warm, soft,
infinite blue reaches
of the understory of life.
We thus might
justifiably assume
that as you walked away,
gazing back
toward our grieving faces
with loving concern,
as far as your attack

upon the path ahead
as it dissolved
before the impenetrable emptiness
of the great divide,
there was no fear
in your stride.
You were going home.

You wanted to stay here
and continue to heal the wounded,
and yet you will not be out of place
in those other, loftier climes.
But we're here on flat earth
in our middle class
world of relative comfort,
eating every day,
sleeping indoors at night,
reading of fatal shootings,
squirming in dentists' chairs,
casting losing votes,
and gauging just how quickly,
at the approach of a monster truck
or a drunkenly weaving
neon-orange painted
Uber electric bike,
we ought to dart across the street.

From time to time,
we look up
and watch for fading
in the impression
that you left behind,

for decay in the airborne **MRI**
printed in copper conductive ink
and washed in lavender light
with hints of peach,
the after image of you
which appears
on thin substrates,
on layered tissues
of cool, coastal fog.
Thus overlaid
on moving masses
of unseen air,
your imprint reveals
a supple spine
in constant lean
toward the mellifluously strumming,
ruby-striated, pomegranate-seed-red,
ever-opening heart of the Divine.

Glory

You knew something
about the Great Mother
that I, like a fool,
never tried to find out.
And now I will never know.
The air around you was so suave
with peace, your passions
so peppered with perspicacity,
your humor so ready a well
of appreciation for what was
then the now
that I forgot to ask.
There was an equilibrium
about you
that was not stasis,
causing time
to bow away
for a moment
when you had something to say.
It was a lightly borne,
unclaimed gravitas
more *intime* in tone,
more svelte in volume,
and of a softer golden light
than that of the possession
of the kingdom,
the power,
and the glory
mentioned
in the doxology

to the Pater Noster.

Glory in you was
of the daily kind-
a gentle, devoted regard
for Yeshua's deep
hemorrhaging of love.

Perhaps his internal rupture
caused a subcutaneous
hematoma of light
to form just under the places
where we walk,
at the crumbled edges
of the divine.
Perhaps that blistering of interior light
is part of the unevenness
of our buckled asphalt lanes
and of footpaths staggering
alongside our railroad tracks,
those zig zag trails
scattered with
chunks of basalt,
that black trap rock
laid out by Southern Pacific
and now strewn with shards
of beer-bottle-brown,
Perrier-Green,
cheap-whiskey-clear,
Vodka-cobalt-blue,
and Bombay-Sapphire-Gin-aqua glass.
Perhaps there are deposits of auric light

bulging under the scratches in the dirt
where lithe coyotes,
glossy raccoons,
pink-faced opossums,
humans who wave at one another
in a truncated way,
ball-capped heads down,
and homeless wanderers walk.

It may be that a wineskin
full of numinous light
began to leak,
bleeding upward
from below the soil
whenever you listened
to Yeshua's blood flowing
beneath it.
Perhaps that was why
in the air round about your head
there was often an aureole of light sensation,
as if whoever was walking with you
was invited to attend
a party of young breezes
disporting themselves
as you, in a resting state,
turned a curve of ear
to the strains of the Divine
singing with its life
to our inattentive world.

On Being Reclaimed by the Truistic

The Worm Moon rose
clear-edged, loosely draped
in trailing yardages of chiffon mist
with no fewer than five planets
transiting before it.
Being weak and fatigued,
I missed it.
However, I did view
a French film
in which two people
pressed their palms
against wind-scoured bricks
on the walled-up portals
of two sacred buildings,
a monastery in Syria
and a small, steep-roofed church
in the French alps.

The air around me has grown opaque,
the outline of your form more vague
as your day of departure
slips back
into the indurating past.
Now it seems that more often
than my dreams are coming true,
my clichés are getting the last laugh.
The ragged grief that once,
head raised,
crawled on hands and knees
over blank terrain

like a black-ink desert wanderer
in a New Yorker cartoon
has now retired
to an upholstered wing chair
and is sighing out worn aphorisms
as quotation-marked
smoke rings
laid out diagonally upon tired air:
"The only thing that is constant
is change." (Heraclitus);
"'Tis better to have loved and lost,
than never to have loved at all."
(Alfred, Lord Tennyson),
and "You are the better part of me." (Jon Secada)
The problem is that these theorems have proven correct.
And the proof is in the insipid
pudding of thought that remains
at the base of my cranial bowl.
While you have become your essential self,
almond-shaped,
as slimly elliptical
as the inner seed
hidden
in the stone
of an apricot,
I have become
emptiness holding
a hard pod
which is sloughing off
brown strings of thought
and flaking away
hackneyed verbal debris.

Once we were
in this thick-skinned
casing together,
two within the aril
awaiting birth.
Since it is frowned upon
to walk away from oneself
in disgust
and to view one's survival
without thanksgiving,
I must hold
our discarded husk
in both hands
with the attitude with which
the French film actors
pressed their palms
to the mortared barrier,
knowing that something
that is evanescent here
but permanently palpable
in timelessness elsewhere
was once within.
The actors knew that
once,
ascending upon
small heat streams
issuing from
guttering candles,
drawn by the lemon scent
of blossoms of holiness,
and rising toward those
open five-petalled flowers,

once there had been
a transparent, bluish
resin-scented brume,
a vaporous effusion
turning sylphlike,
winding upward,
extending its hands outward
in leafy arabesques,
twining upon
the rising prayers
of long-robed priests,
cleaving to the pleas
of desperate pilgrims
coated in dust,
and breathing along with
the whispered words
of quietly, yet persistently faithful
parishioners in work clothes,
a vaporous element
that the mind would frame
with rude two-by-fours of terms
like "cognition" and "mentation"
but that was composed
of the secret thoughts
of the pure of heart,
the unknown visions
of traveling souls.

The Weather

Here, where you were of late,
the air is 54 degrees with a chill wind.
The heavens are populous
with cumulus clouds
fulsomely hillocked.

Dark forested mountains,
new green buds,
and vines all rise
against a sky
saturated with violet, turquoise,
and golden light,
nature as originally made
by the generous,
open-palmed, pagan Creator
who, exchanging one gender
for another and reclining upon clouds,
exhibited the masculine musculature
of the Renaissance
then seemed
to rest in splendid retirement
while being ponderously praised
for centuries in foursquare hymns,
until the April 8, 1966
cover of Time magazine
asked, "Is God dead?"

The shallow sky
above our grocery's parking lot
is frescoed with flowering jessamine,

every vine painting
upon the air
visual panpipe rills played
in a persistent, reedy timbre
with tender, yet determined stems
bearing lanceolate leaves
and pale, yellow flowers.
Asway on suave seacoast breezes,
the jessamine vines now bend,
bowed by buoyantly alighting singing birds.

Across town,
in an open field,
monarch butterflies congregate
in rangy,
altitudinously tall,
yellow-flowered
eucalyptus trees.
In backyards, daffodils,
whom Wordsworth
discovered laughing,
have come and gone,
and the gnarled plum tree
unfolded its stiff paper flowers
some time ago.
Having fallen,
the plum tree's small petals
separately and flatly dot
the callously cold
cement below.
The tissue-thin
white oblongs

are blank fingerprints
left a half a century ago
by the quick,
curious fingers
of the ghost
of your four-year-old self.

The world is anxious to thrive,
but there are still days
when a lead-dark cloud lake
stands fathoms over
our smoking chimneys,
steely drafts
diving deep below
its unseen upper surface
to slip through gaps
in our window and door frames.
It appears that this lake,
using its sullen ominosity,
wishes to discourage
springtime's airborne drifts
of cottonwood fluff
and its innumerable,
ungovernable burstings
of foliate packets,
shouting seedpods
of grasshopper-green
whose pointed lips pull back
to call out foolish promises
of fruit to come,
the seedpods silently exploding
with pink, red, orange, and yellow petals,

and blasts of flaxen pollen.

Your mother has gone home
to the island paradise
where you laughed as a child
before, at the age of five,
you were flown
on a plane to far away
New York.

Almost five decades
after that plane ride,
in fact, this morning,
she walked by herself
to the marketplace
to buy papayas
and soursops.
At home now,
she can feel
the emptiness
of your room.
Your oils are
in small bottles there.
When she opens them,
your room smells like you again.
When they're sealed,
there is a silent vacuum
where you once were.
That vacated space is also
palpable as a physical nothing,
here, out west,
and four thousand miles north.

It seems both unfeeling
and outright wrong
of your room
to have outlasted you,
when those walls know full well
of the amplitude of room
for you
in us.

The Pesky Question of Now

Though you have gone,
sorrow at your passing goes on.
It seems that time and change
have slinky moves.
They fast-step
in vintage sharkskin derbies
with well-waxed hardwood floors
on their side.
But in the small square of time
wherein we box step,
we take a tentative forward step,
and failing to make progress,
we slip to the side;
retreating into sorrow again,
we falter forward,
but again, we slide off to the side.
Finally, forcing ourselves anew,
we manage
a single step
forward.
And all the while,
time and change are jitterbugging
around us,
slide-footing just ahead
then twirling backward,
spinning farther
and farther
behind us
into the irretrievable past.
And it is just these expert antics

of time and change
that seem to be to blame
for causing our own now
to slide forward into our next,
making our next into a now,
making the new now
rather quickly become a past then.
Time and change may turn
our living breath
into a digitally transmitted,
sepia-tinted image of mist
posted somewhere online,
but, for us, whether we're dead or alive,
they can never make you
into a "she," or a "was,"
a "back when," or a "then."

The View

Some believe
that icons are
windows
through which,
praying,
one can see into heaven.
As a metal-framed icon,
you have not changed
since those few days
after you died,
not since those first days
when your eyes,
which had been gazing downward
in the blurry photograph,
turned upward
to look straight across at us,
and your face came into focus
of its own accord,
emanating a reassuringly golden glow.
Your picture has not changed
since then,
but the rectangular,
aluminum-framed view
we see through
through the window
thoughtlessly displaying
its fortune of large transparency
next to our small
photo of you
which stands upon

a black-painted shelf,
continually modifies itself
according to linear time.
Through the aluminum-framed window,
we can see dirt- and petal-carpeted cement,
the back of a weathered board fence,
and above it,
more prosperous, modern,
white-vinyl-framed windows.
The edges of this
aluminum-sided view
are changing
in growing increments
every day.
Just last night,
I noticed that the woody,
five-leaved cane
of a wild raspberry vine
is trying to make the right side
of the empty aluminum box of light
into half of a bosky arch
by tilting itself
across
the window frame's
vertical
line.
And on the left,
from below the sill,
jasmine tendrils
have woven upward
to inscribe y's
whose serifs

are hands formed
of pliant,
reddish, new leaves
held palms open
to the sky.
Jasmine is writing
the beginnings of yeses,
using its deceptively
weak strength
to lead us
away from the
ending of winter
into an unstoppable spring.
Cellulose gears are turning
toward a long summer
which is expected to be
fierce in the mountains
with dangerous heat.
Here, on the coast,
baby boomers
in Patagonia fleeces
walk on streets
and sidewalks alongside
or behind
their dogs,
momentarily escaping
the Covid-19 quarantine.
But you, who,
just last year,
were younger
than they are now,
died

in that season
when medieval Christmas carols
had been recursively chiming,
illustrating the siren-streaked winter air
with solemn, placid virgins,
and with wise men riding camels
and garbed in turbans
and robes of cloth of gold,
as well as with merry gentlemen who,
with maroon-velvet-sleeved arms,
raised full tankards
to their wet, red, rejoicing lips.

Now we can't see you
through our house's front windows
as once we could.
You are not stepping among
the fleece-clothed dog walkers,
swathed in your many
hand woven shawls and scarves,
setting out with careful,
slightly forward-tilting stride
for the organic foods store
to buy more vegetables for juicing.
Your early passing does not seem right.

But I gaze
at our picture-framed view
of you as you are in heaven,
thinking that it was lucky
that you passed
peacefully when you did,

breathing freely
instead of living into the beginnings of spring,
when, given the state of your health,
you probably would have caught
the coronavirus
as it spread hereabouts,
trellised by handshakes,
mundane purchases,
and kisses.
The virus would have,
no doubt,
led to your death
by suffocation.
Since it goes without saying
that your early
and unwilling demise
suffocated something in us,
I won't say it.

Months after your death,
our everyday lives are more distant in time
from nativity scenes
than they are
from hot cross buns,
and on the Indian subcontinent
where you once lived,
Holi has come and gone.
Here, Saint Patrick's Day has passed.
In Rome, the pope has given
his *Urbi et Orbi* address
to an empty St. Peter's Square,
and the Christian world

is far into Lent.
Winter here is over.
Yet, inwardly,
I can still see the bottom rung
of the silk slipper-polished ladder,
the ascending chords
of *O, Come All Ye Faithful.*
I have tied rustic twine
to that first G Major chord,
trellising to that rung
a green creeper of hope
that on the other side
of this transient
coming of spring,
you, with your gentle strength,
your gaze deep as obsidian
and quietly afire
like polished mahogany
in an eternal afternoon of sun,
are indeed joyful,
and triumphant.